The Art of Swinging

A Guide for Beginners

By: Justin F. Green

Dedication:

This book is dedicated to the people who are curious about being curious.

Overview: A look at swinging for people who are curious, have questions, or are debating if swinging is for them.

Purpose: For all intents and purposes, it is safe to say that sexual activities that are outside of the scope of society's opinion of normal sexual prowess are not for everyone. Seemingly, one might be fully comfortable with having a threesome, but cringe at the idea of attending a swinger's party. On the other hand, one might find a swinger's party acceptable, exciting, and impersonal, thus living along the lines that the act of swinging is "just sex." These same people who think a swingers' party is acceptable may cringe or even become enraged at their partner's suggestion of a threesome or one-on-one sex with another person outside of the party element, citing that it is too personal.

These examples reinforce the initial purpose of the statement, that different or abnormal sex, freaky and/or multiple partnered sex is not for everyone. It is important to remember that swinging can be very exciting and a super turn-on for a relationship, but be warned, swinging can also tear down a relationship, and can be the beginning of the end of your friendship/relationship. This book will serve as a guide for couples and singles in all walks of life - for the beginners that want to take baby steps, and for the vets who want to let it all hang out. If you come across a chapter or topic that makes you cringe or you do not feel comfortable with, then that could be a sign that swinging is not for you. Take a deep breath, and take your first step toward *The Art of Swinging.*

Table of Contents

1

How to Swing

What, Why, Where, and When to Swing

How- There are literally two ways to do this. The first way is to just do it! Don't read anything, don't talk about it, just do it and hope for the best. See if your relationship can stand it and deal with the results of it later. Sit back and play witness to what happens due to a night of meaningless playful bliss.

The second way is to read this book and talk to your partner about swinging. You should discuss your wants, your fears, your issues behind swinging, why you want to swing, and what possible benefits you can foresee for you and your partner. Read the Appendix and answer all questions honestly. After reading, answering questions, and talking with yourself and your partner, then the both of you will evaluate the pros and cons and decide if you want to open Pandora's Box.

What- What is swinging? Swinging means different things to different people. For some it means choosing another couple that you know well and trust, or don't know at all to engage in sexual intercourse or engage in sexual behaviors with. Some people view swinging as having a relationship with another couple that could evolve into an alternative relationship where you have your spouse/partner, and also have a boyfriend or girlfriend on the side.

Swinging is unique to the individual and the couple because sex is very personal. Swinging is what you make it and what you adapt as your definition of swinging. However, swinging is not to be confused with cheating. Swinging is not cheating. Swinging is about telling the truth, being honest, and letting your partner know all you do. It's providing a full disclosure. Along with a full disclosure, you have to fully accept the swinging relationship if you chose to indulge in the lifestyle.

Why- Why swing? Why have sex with another person you don't know or barely know? Why have sex with someone other than your partner? Is it to satisfy a need or urge to cheat? Is it purely entertainment?

Some people smoke, while others go to movies, dinner, sports bars, or clubs for entertainment. Others enter the lifestyle of swinging purely as a means of entertainment, fun, and excitement. Only you know what drives or excites you, what makes you want the touch of another woman or man, or both. Whatever the reason, only the individual knows which is one reason why swinging is so mysterious and intriguing.

For some people, the reason to swing or have sex with other people is simple. It is a desire to break a continuous cycle of the same thing over and over. People get stuck in their routines day in and day out. Their lives are the same, sex is the same, and positions are the same. Sexual habitation occurs and people get bored. This cycle of repetitiveness leads to undesired changes in interaction, whether it is someone you're just have sex with or a spouse. It is no secret that after time the intensity of a relationship fades. A simple look, a tilt of the head with a sexy stare or glance, that song one use to sing, the way he or she touched you to make you hot and ready, simply does not do the trick any longer. There is no answer why this happens. It just does because it's a natural occurrence in and out of the bedroom. For some people this occurrence is a fast process, while for others it takes years.

Nevertheless, when sexual habitation occurs, it takes more stimulation to make you hot and ready like before with your partner(s). This is when individuals or even couples look for different sexual experiences for fulfillment. Such things include counseling, hobbies, toys, play dates, role-play, exhibition, pornographic material or other things used to provide stimulus to the relationship. Swinging is no different. It may be a possibility for some to consider because it provides sexual variety and adventure.

For you and your partner, it could be a different reason. Only you know why. Whatever the reason, just be sure you know what you're getting yourself into.

Where- Where can you swing? You can swing anywhere. Swinging by any means is sex. As we all know, sex can take place anywhere, but because swinging usually involves three or more people. The likelihood of the places such as hoods of cars, backseat of a Ford or Chevy, or places that are more comfortable for two people is extremely rare, but not unheard of. The more logical answer would be at home, at someone else's house, hotels, vacations destinations, or at swingers' parties (events or clubs). There are so many different kinds of parties that take place, there is always something that peaks one's interest.

Think of swinging as an art. It is what you make it. You can throw things together and make a mess of it and your life or you can turn your desire into a craft, and your life into a canvas of endless and blissful possibilities.

There are many kinds of swingers' parties- adult pool parties, outdoor exhibitionist parties, house parties, hotel parties, club parties, cabin parties, lake parties, boat parties, themed parties, and even parties where you take trips. The answer is truly anywhere you want, whether it's legal or illegal. A person can find the thrill they are looking for.

When- When do you swing? Everyone is different and the rate in which a person participates in appropriate, legal, or illegal adult activities (swinging and/or threesomes) is up to the individual. Some people swing nightly, weekly, monthly, or a couple times a year. It is really up to the individual/s. The individual must know what they want, what they can live with, and what they can deal with. I urge you to do what you feel is most appropriate for you and your partner.

2

The Six Rules

In life, there are rules we call laws. As in life, these rules were put in effect to protect the majority as well as the individual who participates in swinging. However, just as in life when rules are broken there are consequences. Some are severe and some are minor. This is the reason why people who are considering stepping in the lifestyle of swinging should abide by these rules.

1. Be honest about your sexual preferences.
2. Be honest with your partner.
3. Communicate verbally.
4. If you make a mistake tell you partner.
5. Always, always, always use protection.
6. Respect the person you have sex with (partner and/or invited guest).

Rule 1: Be honest about your sexual preferences.

In layman's terms, your sexual preference is what you want/like. It is also what you want/like to see happen to another person or to yourself. This definition sums up your sexual preference. Once you fully understand what your sexual preferences are, the easier it will be for you to know what you're willing to do inside and outside of your bedroom. I suggest writing them down so you can determine what your wants, your needs, and desires are.

This brings us to "realistic vs. fantasy" sexual preferences. Realistic preferences are what you can stand to actually do and witness in real life. What you are comfortable having done to you. Though some fantasies do come true, I strongly urge you to stay grounded in reality.

Fantasy sexual preferences are the things that you want to see or want to happen in a perfect world, time, place, and setting. I word it like this because a perfect world does not exist, so it would behoove you to understand. In a perfect world people are in control of their feelings, people don't get jealous in a perfect would, people don't cheat in a perfect would, and people don't hurt you or your feelings in a perfect world. So be careful what you ask for because we do not live in a perfect would, and you do have feelings, expectations, dreams, hopes and desires that can be crushed by a loved one, whether it's intentional or unintentional.

Here are a couple of examples to help illustrate the difference between fantasy preferences and a realistic preferences:

Example one - There are some men who like to watch pornographic material of women having sex with well-endowed men. In your mind, this is what you would like to see happen to others because that's what you enjoy seeing in the pornographic material that you watch. There are literally thousands of kinds of pornographic material, and the kinds of material that you chose are normally the kind that you like. It is your choice, your preference, and no judging. However, here is where the confusion comes in. You write your preferences down and you and your partner go over it. In your mind, the actions that you look at in the pornographic material is what you like seeing. In your partner's mind, because you have gone over these things together, she has gotten an understanding that not only are you comfortable with her having sex with well-endowed men, but that you would actually enjoy seeing it, as well. This is an example of fantasy preferences. You like it on the pornographic material that you watch, and may even want to view it at a party, however realistically you may or may not want to see your partner taking on such a large task. Most men do not want their play area damaged or the customized fit knocked lose. So in this example we look at how we have to understand what we really want done to us, or want to be done to our mates. Having this clear understanding of what the difference is between realistic and fantasy preferences will stop arguments, fights, and breakups over misunderstandings.

You have to remember your partner is not a mind reader, and you are not telepathic. You have to spell it out for your partner what you want and don't what. By leaving it up in the air, you open yourself up for potential misunderstandings. If you tell your partner what you truly want and your partner ridicules you, then he or she is not mature enough to engage in the conversation. If they cannot openly have a conversation with you about your preferences or their preferences, then that is, and always will be the determining factor in letting you and your partner know that this lifestyle is not for the two of you. It may be for you or it may be for them, but it is not for the both of you together. This will be the time for you to make a choice to go forth with entering the lifestyle as swingers or not.

Still reading? Good. Since you're still reading, we will continue with sexual preferences. Your sexual preferences define what you will allow or not allow in your bedroom.

Another issue associated with sexual preference is labeling. Straight, gay, bisexual, transsexual, etc., are all labels. What label do you fall under? These labels differ for everyone because there are so many different ways to define one's sexuality.

If you are a woman and you have a threesome with another woman and a man, what label defines you? In talking with others all would agree and still consider the woman to be straight, depending on the activities that took place during the threesome. What does this mean? It means that just because a threesome consists of another woman, interaction between the females does not have to take place. Now, depending on what takes place, a woman can engage in sexual activities with another female, and then the woman would then fall into the category of bisexual or bi-curious. However, if you are a male, and you have a threesome with a female and another male, most people will say the male is 100% straight. Again, this depends on if there was penetration between the males during the threesome. If this happens, some may feel a bit confused on if the male is gay or bisexual.

Is there a such thing as a bisexual male? It is hard to classify a male as bisexual because society does not see men in this form. Society sees men as either gay or straight. The men in this classification will argue and say that they are bisexual because they like and enjoy the full pleasures of being with women and men, but society sees them as homosexual. What is difficult to assess is what the term gay really means. Is there a line that separate the two? Do we say bisexual as a means of justification from being ridiculed sexually or do some people actually believe that bisexual is not the same as being homosexual?

Let's break it down. Straight sex is sexual intercourse or behaviors performed with the opposite sex. Most will not argue with this definition because the answer is straight forward.

Homosexual means that a person enjoys having sex with a person of the same sex, and only of that sex. They do not wish to, or enjoy having sex with persons of the opposite sex.

Bisexual is defined as a person who enjoys sexual intercourse with the same sex and people of the opposite sex equally. Sex does not need to be accompanied by the opposite sex at all to fulfill sexual gratification.

Bi-curious is an individual who enjoys the full pleasure of the opposite sex, but is unsure of all the things that they like or enjoy about the same sex. Sexual encounters are still preferred to be with the opposite sex, but the person still enjoys the thought of being with another person of the same sex, or even enjoy having sexual intercourse with someone of the same sex.

Let's dig deeper. Straight, bisexual, bi-curious, and homosexual all seem to be straight forward. But are they? Are the terms specific to everyone? Does the term straight correlate to a man having sexual relations with a transsexual? Most would say no, but, why not?

It could then be argued that my prior definition of straight would not only be lacking specifics, but would need to be defined for men as, "engaging in vaginal intercourse with a woman born as a woman." The reason for the specification of the definition is because what you believe also plays a factor in what or who you are. If a transsexual man he is a woman, and the man believes that she is a woman, how do you define the interaction of sex?

 Mentally the man as had sex with what he feels is a woman, and the said woman has had sex with a man. However, in this case the man is classified as bisexual and the transsexual is classified as gay. How you ask? Remember the term bisexual is defined as, "enjoying sexual relations or intercourse with the same sex and people of the opposite sex equally." So even though a man just had sex with a man (transsexual), he still feels that the sex was performed with a woman. Genetically, the woman was a male, so it is assumed that the male enjoys having sex with males as well as females. Thus the male is labeled as bisexual. The transsexual is considered gay or homosexual because although he views himself as a woman, he is still only engaging in sex with other males which defines the transsexual as gay.

If the transsexual is post-op, meaning he no longer has a penis and now has a vagina, the male that engages in sex with the transsexual is now considered straight, if he is unknowing of the transsexual's birth gender, and the transsexual is now considered bisexual. Why? Again, remember what you believe plays a factor in your sexual orientation. If the male does not know his partner was once a man, then he is straight. He has to want or like having sex with men to be bisexual or homosexual. The transsexual by law is now a female, her body is regulated with estrogen, and he believes it is a female as well. Because of the law, and because physically she now is a female, then she is now bisexual because "she" is having sex with only men, but genetically she is still a male, and chemically she is a female. This is just a general rule of thumb and not considered a fact because again only you can determine your label or your sexual preference/orientation.

Be careful with labeling. Make sure you are honest with yourself and your partner about your true feelings and desires. Once you're honest about this, the level of sexual pleasure will increase between yourself and people you chose to be sexually intimate with. You will no longer have to hide your sexual desires. What was once limited, can now be explored openly.

Finally, I cannot stress this enough, be honest about your orientation and preferences. If you're a male and likes having a finger inserted your booty for you to climax, say it. If you are a woman who likes to be choked a little or have your hair pulled, say it. I know that may sound a little out there to some, but to others these are tactics that turn them on in the bedroom. Although these are all just examples, there are many different things that work for many different people. The trick is knowing what works for you and your relationship (preference).

Rule 2: Be honest with your partner.

Someone once said honesty is the best policy. In the swinging world, it is the only policy. You will undoubtedly meet people who are liars and cheats. Some people will lie about everything, from their name, height, weight, pants size, relationship status, age, STD/HIV status, endowment, breast size, and how sexually active they are. Sadly this is told before you have sex with them. Just imagine what lies they will tell you during your sexual encounter or after. If you happen to fall prey to their lies and have a relationship with them, I suggest cutting them off because it will only get worst.

What can you do to avoid the lies affecting you? My advice is to do what you do in your normal every day, non-sexual life. Get to know a person first. Know some of their likes and dislikes. Start a conversation. Ask them specific questions about themselves, and don't be afraid to ask for proof, especially age if you like younger women. Love yourself enough to know the truth, and protect yourself. This goes for single people and for couples.

This rule applies for all types of adult parties as well. Though you will likely never see this person again (unless you exchange information), it is still your responsibility to live up to your standards. We all have to set standards for ourselves. It does not matter if you're in a new or strange situation. Your standards should not deter from what they normally are. If you normally require people to prove they are single or disease free, then there should not be a difference in this process whether it is a threesome, a swinger's party, or someone you want to engage in a relationship with. Respect yourself, and be honest with yourself and with your partner.

With your partner, honesty is key! It can be the pillar or corner stone that holds your relationship together. Honesty can get you your cake, and you can eat it too, if you just tell the truth. Your partner will respect you for your candidness and honesty. If you put 100 percent trust in your partner and lay everything on the table, do everything within the confines of your relationship, always ask permission, put her or his feelings and respect before yours, then your relationship will evolve. Someone once asked what is the benefit(s) to being a swinger and having a relationship based on this lifestyle? The answer is evolution. Now, I'm not saying you cannot get evolution without a swinging/lifestyle type relationship, but you can be sure that going down this road and surviving will leave your relationship unbreakable.

**** Caution****

The vast majority of relationships that enter into this lifestyle do not survive. When I say vast, I will be bluntly honest and tell you that your relationship will probably not make it through this lifestyle. It's sad to say, but it is true. Entering into the lifestyle of swinging will allow your partner to see you in a whole new light. The vast majority do not like the new view. However, if you are "lucky" (yes I said lucky), your relationship will become stronger because of it. I will go as far as saying that your relationship could evolve into an "unbreakable" one; a relationship that is strong, and easily resembles the one depicted in the movie, "*The Notebook*."

Telling your partner the truth can enhance your relationship not only inside of the bedroom, but outside of the bedroom. Truth be told, the number one reason for relationships failing is settling. Settling for the bullshit, for the half-truths, for the lies, for the cheating, for the lack of faith and the lack of effort. This does not have to be the case. Relationships have and can make it through these times of uncertainty. All you have to do is have a little faith, and be honest with your partner. When you're honest in one area it is easier to be honest about all aspects of your relationship. You bring forth a line of communication that very few relationships get to experience. You will become better friends. You will gain a new respect for each other. You will respect your partner for their opinions, their honesty, their presence, their patience, and even for sticking it out with you.

Rule number two is easier said than done, yet people always say they want the truth. It is my opinion that it can be hard for people to be totally honest with their partners. We as people can blame lying on any number of things.

I believe that the simple innate nature of self-preservation enables us to lie without thought, to preserve one's self. As a child, we lied to avoid trouble. This in fact is one of the very first moments that we comprehend the gravity of preservation. To tell the truth and get in trouble, or to lie and there be a possibility to escape punishment, whether it be minor or severe. It is for this innate reason that I believe it is rare for a person to be totally honest with their mate on all levels. Rare does not mean that honest relationships do not exist. In fact, rare in this case means, for the few that do step out on a leap of faith and commit to being honest all the time, their relationship becomes special. This type of relationship is rarely seen.

The same rule of being honest with your partner is the same reasoning and same approach you must take when evaluating whether or not you wish to participate in having a threesome, attending a party, or even just deciding to become involved in the swinging lifestyle in any aspect. If you realize this is not for you after being honest with your partner, there is no shame. There will be several points throughout the book that will help you to decide on what you want to do next. You may choose that this lifestyle is not for you, or you may choose to move forward with swinging. Let honesty be your guide and if at the end of this book you decide that swinging is not for you then follow your gut. Please, please, please don't make the mistake of doing it for the sole purpose of making your partner happy. Make sure both parties are in agreement about moving forward with whatever decision you make. You owe it to yourself and your partner to be honest with your feelings.

Rule 3- Communicate verbally.

There are many ways to communicate. A smile, a hand gesture, body language, silence, eye movements, even a stare with your eyebrows frowned speaks volumes. All of these are ways that people communicate with others, but all these ways of communication can be misinterpreted, except for verbal communication. Though verbal communication can be misconstrued at times, if you speak clearly and directly stating precisely what you are talking about without slang or double meaning words, then the subject matter will not be lost in translation. Remember, "Everything is open to interpretation until you open your mouth." (Keshia Green)

Example: A couple decides to have a threesome with a female. All three retreat to the bedroom for an evening of blissful fun. In prelude to intercourse the male counterpart of the couple decides to go down on the invited female. The female counterpart of the couple has often talked about seeing him go down on a woman and wanting to watch. The male, without asking, sees this as an opportunity to not only indulge himself, but to also satisfy his woman's desire by fulfilling "her" fantasy of watching him feast on another woman. During the process of going down on the invited woman, the female counterpart of the couple realizes she cannot stand to see her man eat another woman out. Instead of telling the male counterpart to stop, she gives cues throughout the process. Because the male counterpart is enjoying himself, he misses the subtle cues. As you can guess this is a big problem.

The female counterpart is mad at the male counterpart for an action that took place that was seemingly not his fault. Or was it his fault?

Should he have been more in tune with his female counterpart than the invited guest?

Making your female counterpart, whether she is a friend, girlfriend, or wife feel less important than the invited guest is a sure fire way to end all swinging experiences. This situation is both of their faults. It was the man's fault for assuming that this was what his woman/partner wanted, and not asking her directly. It was the female's fault for not speaking up and telling him to stop.

In the heat of the moment very few people think rationally when they feel jealous and it is interpreted as them being angry, upset, emotionally hurt, insulted, or betrayed. When you talk about what happened during or after, it is important to be calm and rational. Adding frustration, anger, or other emotions to a serious conversation is always a bad idea.

Think about it, where have you ever seen people having a conversation where one or both became emotional, and the conversation turn out good? If you want your point to be heard, you have to be calm. Your relationship is your business, so make the conversation a business meeting. Keep it professional.

Like in the example above, this and an array of other potential problems can all be avoided by following this simple rule: Communicate verbally before, during, and after the sexual experience! The army has a technique they use to modify and correct things that go wrong after an exercise, event, or task. They call it an AAR (After Action Review). I strongly suggest couples or friends adapt to this form of communication because it will increase the sexual experience by making future encounters flow without problems. An AAR is simply putting your feelings out there about the experience. You give three positive notes on a topic, then three negatives (if there were any). Then you review both the bad and the good. After reviewing, you plan on how to avoid the negative things that occurred in the future.

Example: A couple invites a female to participate in a threesome. During the course of the threesome the invited female squirted all over your bed. Though exciting, you just realized that this invited guest peed all over your bed. Not cool for several reasons that we don't need to go into or point out. Afterward, the couple performs an AAR and discuss how to avoid this situation from reoccurring. They come up with the following:

> A) The couple can just simply tell the next woman they invite that no squirting allowed.

> B) The couple could have the next sexual encounter take place at a hotel or at the invited woman's house.

> C) The couple could screen future invited guest to ensure they find a woman who does not climax in such a manner.

After picking A, B, or C. The couple follows through by sticking to which ever choice they decide. To ensure the process of having a 3sum is an enjoyable one.

Though these are just examples, it is important that couples and singles understand that people are not mind readers, nor telepathic.

It is easy to get upset with someone and infer what they should have known. This is not me telling you how to think or how your relationship should go, but again your relationship and life will run smoother if you follow this rule. Always communicate verbally.

Rule 4- If you make a mistake tell your partner.

This might be the hardest rule to follow because it's more than telling the truth or communicating verbally. Nobody wants to hear the proverbial words of "I told you so." Nobody wants to admit that someone else was right, or that they did something wrong. However, to be in this lifestyle you have to be accustomed to telling the truth. If you get caught lying, I can honestly say it will be the beginning of the end of the two of you swinging, if not the end of your relationship altogether.

You can make a mistake and tell the truth, and have a better outcome than lying about the incident or mistake. Making a mistake does not mean you have cheated. Every relationship is going to develop its own rules and guidelines whether they are implied or written down and mounted on a wall somewhere. Follow your rules, and if you break one let your partner know. This rule is simple. If you make a mistake tell your partner, don't lie.

Rule 5- Always, always, always use protection.

This rule is about respect. Respect for yourself and respect for others. This rule is important because it covers hygiene. Many people think that just because you use protection at a party you are safe from the spread of potential bacterial diseases as well as sexually transmitted diseases. This is not the case. Women are typically the cleanest, but they are more susceptible to bacteria and sexually transmitted diseases.

Most women after each sexual experience go to the restroom to freshen up. This includes washing of the vaginal area, along with new perfume, mouthwash and other things to clean one's self up. Even though this is occurring she is still as likely to get a STD as if she did not wash at all. Why?

The answer is simple. Most men do not wash up after each sexual encounter. After hosting nearly 100 parties I have seen three men (including myself), wash up after each play session. When a male wears a condom, it protects him from getting a STD because the opening of his urethra is at the tip of his penis, allowing the condom to prevent access of foreign bodies into his body.

When a man has sex with a woman, body fluid gets on the shaft and base of the penis, along with the pelvic area. When this occurs the body fluid typically dries fast when exposed to air. After a sexual encounter a man removes the condom after use, finds another woman to have sex with and applies another condom for intercourse. In his mind, and the mind of the second woman that he has decided to have sex with, he is being responsible, but because he did not wash up, the body fluid from the first female is still on his body (shaft and pelvic area). When he begins to have sex with the second female the application of her body fluid or even sweat, on the once dried body fluid from the first woman is then moistened again. Once the dried fluid is moistened, it can then be passed to the second woman during intercourse. What has just happened is that both the first female and second females' fluids have mixed.

This normally takes place at the base and pelvis region of the male. This is typically accomplished by the fluids mixing and the continuous strokes of the male pushing both fluids back into the opening of the vaginal area. This transference of fluids is a process called female to female transmission of STD's via male. This is rarely thought of which makes women more susceptible to STD's. Sadly, even when the act of female to female transmission of STD's via a male is thought of, it is even rarer for a female to voice her opinion and to simply tell males to wash up before intercourse.

Wearing protection is simply not enough when having sex with multiple partners. Good hygiene alone is not enough. As women, as men, as couples you cannot be scared to voice your concerns, and have the people you chose to play with take precautions in cleaning themselves. People have jobs where they come into contact with all types of germs and bacteria.

Take a mechanic for example. Their hands stay stained and dirty. Now imagine if you would that you are a female and you are a guest at an adult party where sex is occurring. The Mechanic fingered you or other women at this party. You think you're safe because you only got fingered or you only had oral sex (with fingers). Without making the mechanic clean himself up, you have just exposed yourself to a day or even days of potentially fatal bacteria, oil, dirt, sewage, road kill, animal droppings, hazardous waste, grass, pollen, spores, and different kinds of liquids. All of these are potential ways to expose you, all wrapped up in one man's hands because he touches tires and the under panels of cars. Yes, this is a stretch, but it is not far from reality. The same goes for people who work at schools, hospitals, or factories. There is nothing wrong with asking your potential play partners to protect themselves and you by having them wash before sexual activities. Have them wash their hands, and rinse their mouths out with mouth wash along with bathing.

If the examples are not enough, let's get scientific for just a minute. Scientists studying swingers have found that straight couples who regularly swap sexual partners and indulge in group sex at organized events, say that couples have higher rates of sexually transmitted infections (STIs) than prostitutes. Yes, this is a true and a correct statement. In fact, in the study preformed one in ten older swingers had Chlamydia, and around one in twenty had Gonorrhea. In 70 percent of the cases none of the women had symptoms. This is just for straight couples. When bisexual partners are included the numbers rise. Moral of this rule is to protect yourself and others.

Rule 6: Respect for the person you have sex with (partner and invited guest).

Having respect for others is a rule that will save a lot of issues from happening at a party or even in the privacy of your own home. When you respect the person you sleeping with even if you do not know them, you display a sense of security and maturity that allows the persons involved to relax and open up. Think about this, if you invite someone over for a threesome they are going to be nervous maybe even a little scared. Just like if you go to a swingers' party and you're nervous or scared, it's up to the host to make you feel comfortable. So when you invite someone over or if you have sex with someone it's your job to make them feel comfortable. Along with respect comes courtesy. Rule of thumb in this instance is doing unto others as you have them do unto you.

This chapter stresses the importance of these six rules. Individuals and couples should abide by these six rules to have a successful and blissful relationship whether it's a one night stand, casual or serious relationship. The purpose of this book is to serve as a guide for people who wish to indulge themselves into the lifestyle and want guidance. This will help you determine if swinging is for you, and help you understand the dos and the don'ts of the swinging lifestyle.

3

Knowing What You Can Handle and Live With

What is art? Webster's Dictionary defines art as a, "skill acquired by experience, study, or observation." This is also how I define swinging, and thus the title of this guide *"The Art of Swinging,"* was born. Swinging is a craft, a skill, an implication of personal, unanalyzable creative power. The art of swinging is the power to make love, the skill and pose to master your chi, and block or extinguish jealousy. The art of swinging is masterfully basking in the full and undulated pleasures of lust and playful bliss.

Swinging is not a new concept, phase, or fad. Women and men swing all the time, however most people call it cheating because the other partner does not know of the swinging (cheating) that's taking place. The concept of swinging is simple. It is the fundamental design to trust your partner enough to tell the truth, and allow your partner to give you permission to sleep with other people, instead of cheating.

We discussed why people go into the lifestyle of swinging. Some people allow swinging because they love their partner and believe they will cheat anyway, and would rather just know who it is and when they do it. They also believe that if they allow it, it will stop their partner from leaving them. This is a leap of faith, though it works sometimes, it does not work all the time. This is not a reason to swing or have a threesome. Swinging is not for people who cheat, the weak minded or the jealous. It's for the people who have turned their passion for flesh into a craft; an art.

Every artist is different. Each style and technique is different. Each master craftsman or artist scopes his canvas with a rejuvenated form of his or her essence to make up what their lifestyle will encompass. It is important to know what you will not tolerate, can and cannot live with, and can and cannot do.

Knowing what you can handle and live with is the most important step in evaluating whether or not you want to step into the lifestyle of swinging. This book has covered six rules you should abide by, what your preferences are, and in the following chapter you will get some tips on what to do and what not to do. The most important step is to know what you won't do, what is too much for you, and what you can handle and live with.

Establishing rules for yourself and/or your relationship is simple, and most of your rules will come from answering the questions in Appendix A honestly. If the Appendix does not help you formulate your rules, then simply talking to your partner or sitting back and evaluating yourself should help you form some rules. Once you do this, it is important that you stay strong and live by your rules. Do not do anything that you will regret or you feel will undermine who you are as a person. Don't allow yourself to be put in situations where you are forced to comply or do things you do not want to do. Making the decision to participate in the swinging lifestyle is your decision. Your participation should only be because you want to have fun and be adventurous. It should not be because you were forced or talked into it. You will have regrets and guilt if you do it for any other reason than wanting to do it for yourself.

This chapter is designed to help guide you to making rules that suit you and your relationship. It is also to help you realize the importance of your self-worth. You have to establish what you can handle and what you can live with.

4

Party Etiquette

If you have never been to a swinger's party there may be many questions you want to ask and there are things you should know before attending one. This chapter on party etiquette includes information such as what to wear, how to act, avoiding confrontation, and much more. Do not attend a party without reading this chapter.

Invitation - If the party invitation has a RSVP and you plan to attend, make sure you RSVP according to the instructions. Arrive on time. It's not fashionable or polite to show up to a swingers' party late. You run the risk of being turned away, and if not you may make people who have already begun playing feel awkward by coming in late. Also, for those who want to play, when you come late it will be harder for you to fit in, thus harder for you to play with other people at the party. Inform the host ahead of time if you are going to be late for any reason, even if it's just due to traffic. Being courteous goes a long way.

What to do - It's important to have a good time. If you're not having a good time, leave. The night is about you acting out your fantasies and seeing what the lifestyle has to offer. It's more than just sex, swinging and threesomes. You can make friends, network and make some really great connections as long as you have a positive attitude. This should be common sense, but leaving nothing to chance, please put a mint or a piece of gum in your mouth before you walk in the door. First impressions are lasting impressions.

Party rules - Always follow the rules of a party. If you don't follow the rules then you cannot be mad if you are asked to leave or asked to pay more at the door when you arrive the next time. The host will remember you. If there is a theme to a party, whether it is all-white attire, lingerie, pool party, costume party, or you're simply asked to wear a certain color, please abide by the rules. Again if you do not abide by the rules, do not be alarmed if you are either asked to leave, denied entry, or asked to pay more at the door (if attending a paid event).

How to act – This should be self-explanatory whereby the situation dictates the behavior. Some tips on what not to do include, but are not limited to: cursing, obsessive aggressive behaviors, being rude, public drunkenness, or leaving your date for any reason. Typically you should act like you're at an upscale night club or jazz bar. Dressing like you are going out on a nice date will insure you are dressed sexy yet maturely, and will distinguish you from the immature crowds that tend to show up. Take whatever personal items you are going to need with you. Going back and forth to your car makes people nervous. Remember, think about how you would feel. There are a lot of crazy people out there, don't get labeled as one.

If you're staying over or it is a party that lasts "until," carry a small bag for all the little things you may need like lingerie or a robe, hairbrush, comb, toothbrush, cologne, intimate cleansing articles, condoms, etc. Sleeping bags or blankets and pillows are necessities if you think or you are going to stay the night. Keep money, jewelry and other such valuables at a minimum, in fact leave them in the car locked up in your glove box if you can. It's embarrassing to a host if you lose them, not to mention the anger, resentment and other emotions that follow when you lose or believe something has been stolen from you.

Don'ts for Men and Women

•   Don't become a nuisance, typically called a bug-a-b00. A bug-a-boo disturbs others with prolonged talking. They are also known for coming into bedrooms, peeling back curtains, turning on lights, etc. Accidents do happen, but don't become known for being a bug-a-boo. It can be very annoying and kill the mood for other participants. Beware, if you become known for being a bug-a-boo you will find that you won't receive many invites in the future.

•   Don't bring a straggler to a swingers' party. Some refer to them as tickets. A straggler is someone who goes with you to a party just to get in, but has no intention of swinging. This is wrong on many levels because even people who come just to watch are participants. They add to the decor of the party. When you come with another person, it is normally expected that the other one is willing to swing or participate as well. Stragglers are typically easy to pick out because they are uninterested in anything that is going on, and appear to wish to be some place other than at a swingers' party.

•   Don't take someone to a party who is not fully informed. This person is called the uninformed. It is obvious when a person is brought to a party and does not know that they are attending a swingers' party. This is embarrassing for the host, to the unsuspecting person, as well as embarrassing to you depending how the unsuspecting person (the uninformed) takes it. Please understand this has the potential to, and will probably, cause problems.

• Don't do anything that you don't want to do or feel uncomfortable doing sexually. Only do what is fun for you. Do not allow yourself or your partner to become sexually involved with anybody that you are not interested in. Don't force your partner to play with someone else because you want to play with the male or female counterpart of another couple. There is no reason to involve yourself in a scene that you are not comfortable with. You chose to come to a party or involve yourself in a threesome for your enjoyment. So if you are not enjoying yourself opt out and stop. I know this is repetitive, but again, only do what you want, when you want and with whom you want! Doing anything other than that is your fault because you failed to open your mouth and say, "No", "Stop", "I don't want you to do that", "I don't want us to do that", or "I don't want to do that."

• If there is a problem never take the matter into your own hands. This can lead to serious problems such as arguments, violent fights, and law enforcement being called. This does not mean you do not have the option to say, "No", "Leave me alone", or even tell someone to "chill", but the moment it seems like any situation is going to escalate, remember it is not your place, house or event. Show some respect and humility to your host, and allow them to take the situation over. Example - If people are being abusive or not taking no for an answer, unwanted touches, or there is obsessive drunkenness, do not hesitate to tell the host.

•   Don't be unclean. Nothing turns a person off faster and more effectively than an unclean body or stale breath. Even if you shower and perfume yourself before you leave home, it is always a good idea to freshen up again when you arrive at your destination. It is amazing what a little time can do on a drive somewhere (or undo). People stop for a bite to eat or cars may have an odor, so as a precaution take a moment to refresh.

Don'ts for Women

Women are God's gift to man and undoubtedly the best thing to ever happen to men, but at the same time women can be mans' downfall. Women tend to believe they can do no wrong, in and out of the bedroom. This is not the case, and to help you realize this I will lay out some swingers' party don'ts.

•   Absolutely no squirting. For some reason, it has become increasingly more common for women to relax their muscles during sex and release urine during intercourse. It is not to say that cumming or climaxing in the marrer is not possible, but whether you do or you don't climax in this manner it is still unsavory to do so without first seeing if the place you are going to have sex is set up to accommodate water play.

- The act of squirting without proper accommodations and preparations is rude to do at an event or during threesomes. Save squirting for home, or a one-on-one session outside of party events. What you view as an orgasm to some may be viewed as you taking the liberty to just pee on their furniture. If you still don't understand, just imagine someone coming to your house and standing in the middle of your living room and releasing on the floor. This would be unacceptable to you, just as it is unacceptable for someone to release on someone else's bed without permission.

- Again, I am not saying whether it is or is not an organism. Whether it's an orgasm, pee, soda, beer, or any type of fluid, most hosts do not appreciate people ruining their furniture. Have the proper respect and lay a towel down or bed mat made for fluid if this is the only way for you to reach a climax/cum.

- No anal sex. In this environment, you may feel the urge to let loose some of   those built up tabooed desires. It is not recommended that anal sex be one of those urges you explore. Be respectful of others. There are several reasons not to perform anal sex, including: the smell after pulling out, the clean-up, the possible spilling of bowel movements on the floor, the bed or furniture. These things are normally enough to have a reasonable person think twice about the action, but if thinking is not enough, I repeat, do not perform anal sex at a party. During a threesome or one-on-one encounter, this act would be more appropriate.

- It is not okay to come to a swingers' party while your menstrual cycle is on, or if it has just gone off. The law of chaos will occur; everything that shouldn't go wrong will go wrong. You will spot, you will bleed, you will smell, you will get blood on the toilet seat, and you will undoubtedly be embarrassed. If your cycle happens to come on while you are at the party, politely leave. There is no shame, it happens. If you run into a well-endowed man that in layman terms "beats it up," and you began to bleed, or spotting occurs, then the same rule applies and it would be time for you to leave. Round two is not recommended if that occurs. If more is desired, pass your phone number off to him.

You can also leave and meet at a hotel/your home if blood play is your thing.

- Do not arrive intoxicated. It is one thing to be nervous and to be tipsy. If you arrive tipsy, know your limit. Do not continue to drink. Don't be "that girl." The one throwing up everywhere, having sex with twenty men and not even realizing there are different men climbing on top of her. Nobody comes to a party to be a baby sitter. No host wants to go around cleaning up vomit and no host wants police showing up days later for rape charges because you were irresponsible. These are actual occurrences, not what if's. I cannot stress these tips enough. No one wants to clean up pee, feces, blood, or vomit after a party. It's nasty, rude, and so disrespectful.

- If this tip applies to you please take heed and be warned. If it does not apply to you, then don't let it bother you. Don't come to an event with a bad attitude. People come to parties to escape the normalcies of life. It is the same reason people go to bars, clubs, movies, games, and other nonsexual events. People come to events to have fun. People do not come to be faced with rudeness and bad attitudes. If for whatever reason you (women) feel you're too cute to be approached, then a swingers' party is the wrong place for you. If you feel you are unapproachable, I will be the first to tell you that you will be very annoyed at a party because every man, tall, short, skinny, fat, small package to well-endowed, and any race that is at the event will approach at any given time. Do not forget the reason that you and other like-minded people decided to come to the party in the first place.

•   Do not be overly aggressive. Women generally get away with things that men cannot such as touching women, grabbing women, asking repeatedly even when the answer has been no or not interested. This happens a lot, especially with women that like other women. No means no, and stop means and always will mean stop. When you say no, you generally mean it and the woman that you approach means it as well, when she/he/they (couple) says no.

Don'ts for Men

For whatever reason, when men come to their first swingers' party, they are under the impression they are going to have sex with every hot female at the event. This is not the case. Even though you are in an exciting, new environment not to act like a jerk. Acting like a jerk is an easy accomplishment in this environment. You may be labeled as a jerk by being rude, not asking permission, handling a female the wrong way, getting drunk, or just being an asshole. If you like to swing you will have to understand that this is not a label that you want. It is a hard label to get rid of. Although I mention throughout the book that swinging and people in the lifestyle are everywhere (in every state and town), you have to realize it is still a small community and you can make a name for yourself very quickly as the one not to invite to a party. Here are some quick tips to help you stay out of trouble.

- Whether you are well-hung or not, keep your penis in your pants unless it is a dress down party or everyone is walking around naked. Remember even though you may feel you're blessed and want the ladies to know it, there are other men walking around too, and if they don't have to see it, they don't want to see it.

- Do not put your penis in a woman's face. Find a creative way of asking for head, but I promise just taking it out and putting it in someone's face is not going to turn out well. Remember, respect. This rule still applies when you walk in a room and there is an orgy taking place. Even then, keep it in your pants. Go up to the orgy and watch, play, or you can even take your penis out as long as you don't put it in anyone's face.

- Wrap your penis up. If you don't have condoms, ask someone. You do not have an excuse. Always be prepared, even if you go to a party with intentions of just watching you should still have condoms. Also, even if you ask for a condom, you may not get one. Condoms are like cash at a swingers' parties. People do not share so get your own and bring extras.

• Do not touch what is not yours. This includes food, drinks, and women! Remember the rules of the world still apply at a house party, sex party or event. Women can get away with things you can't. A woman can go up to another woman and just touch and feel on another woman with no issues. I do not suggest this for males. Ask first. The man who shows more respect is the man who gets more play at the events.

• Do not flush condoms down the toilet, put them in the trashcan. Don't be the guy to clog the bathroom toilet at someone's house.

• Do not ejaculate on anyone. Your condom should be on at all times anyway. If you do not have a condom on, do not perform this act. Get it out of your head that you are a porn star or that this is a porn movie scene. Those women get paid to be dehumanized or degraded. Very few women like this, and the ones who do are not shy about asking for it. Don't assume. An unclear no means no; a clear and concise yes, means yes.

• Whether you're an Alpha male or not, do not be overly aggressive with women at parties. Assertiveness, confidence, and aggression are all different things, and all three are perceived differently.

Don'ts for Couples

If this is your first party and you came with a partner, do not stray away. It's just like being in a new city or town the environment is confusing and the layout of the event is much easier to navigate together. Find out which areas you don't want to get involved with.

Example - If you're a couple, you may want to stay away from the gang bang rooms, where one woman is taking on the whole house in groups of 2-5 people at a time. Again, this is a good time to remember realistic preference vs. fantasy preference. Trust me you will never look at your partner the same again once she has been in a Mandingo party (gang bang). So again, stay together and explore together. You don't want your lady to get caught up in something she didn't intend, and things happen fast.

Some additional rules to follow:

> •All the don'ts for men and women apply to the couple or playmates as well. The biggest rule is respect. Have respect for yourself and others.

> •Don't invite people into your space unless you are sure that the both of you are secure and ready. It's really weird and uncomfortable for other people when they get caught in your jealousy or insecurities.

> •Don't speak on behalf of your mate. When considering participation, don't dive in without your partner also feeling comfortable.

•Do not arrive as a couple and leave single. Always arrive as a couple and leave as a couple. It will not be viewed favorably if one partner leaves early and the other stays the duration of the party. Simple rule, if one goes, both go. Even if you break up or fight at a party, leave together. No one needs to see or know your business. This will ensure you being invited again whether you stay together or have a new playmate the next time you come.

•The mind has a way of playing tricks on people. To avoid conflicts, I strongly urge couples to stay together. You don't want your partner to disappear for 30 minutes and be enraged because you feel like they have done something and they haven't. Remember, you have not been in this situation or all the situations that can occur. The two of you do not want insecurities or jealousy to sneak up and ruin a party. This is a lifestyle full of people with insecurities, uncertainties, and fears. Just stay in line and remember to stay with your partner.

•The most important rule for couples is not the most obvious. For couples, it is important that you wear protection with each other at parties. Sounds weird, but it is necessary for obvious reasons. Let me point some out.

Example 1 - If the male counterpart of a couple ejaculates inside of the female counterpart, then the female runs the risk of exposing everyone else at the party to different bacterial infections. This takes place several ways.

If another male or female provides oral sex to the female counter part, then she has introduced sperm into the mouths of unsuspecting participants. Nobody wants a mouth full of sperm by way of transport.

Example 2 - If the male counterpart ejaculates inside the female counterpart and then the female counter part decides to have sex with other males, the males' sperm accumulates at the base of another man's penis which can be transmitted to someone else during sex.

As we covered earlier, it is easy for men to transfer STD's by way of transporting fluids from one female to the next. It is odd for most couples to use protection among themselves, but I stress the importance of doing so at parties to minimize the risk of contributing to sexually transmitted diseases and uncleanliness.

This chapter is for people who want to give swinging a try and are not quite sure what to do or not to do. This chapter alone will allow singles and couples to learn some of the ends and outs of swinging. You can almost call this chapter the rule book. I suggest reading this chapter twice.

5

25 Most Frequently Asked Questions

- **How often does a relationship go wrong due to swinging?**

Surprisingly almost all relationships go wrong due to some degree or severity of an offense by one or both partners. How wrong just depends on what occurred to make the relationship go wrong, whether it's cheating, not wanting to stop swinging, cheating inside the parties, lies, or a number of other things. Again, follow the guide, *"The Art of Swinging"* and save some heartache. The guide can lead couples to having a great relationship that incorporates swinging without issues.

- **What is the main reason people swing?**

People swing for any number of reasons, but the most honest answer is because they can.

It is something that not everyone can do, or has the option of doing. The mere conversation or discussion about swinging is exciting. Sometimes the conversation alone is enough to spark some excitement in your relationship. The fact is if you're thinking about swinging or having sex with someone else means there is something going on within yourself or your relationship. This can be a good thing, or a bad thing. Only you can decide.

- **If you have a partner that is not sure about entering or remaining in the lifestyle, how should you handle that?**
Well, this can be handled in three ways. The first of which is to simply not do it. The second is to go for it and see what happens. The third way, which I feel is more practical, is to talk to your partner, reassure them, and make sure they are comfortable. It is your job to make your partner is comfortable with any situation. Whether it's sex, financial problems, career changes, etc. If you cannot instill a sense of security in your partner for the endeavor you wish to take part in, this is a good indication that swinging may be for you, but not for the both of you.

- **If you attend a party and you don't feel sexually attracted to anyone, what do you do?**

This happens frequently with women and occasionally with men. It really depends on your standards. Some people's standards are lower at a swinger's party because it is not their intention to be with the person they have sex with outside of the party. However, some people's standards do not change and finding a partner or people to have sex with at a party can become increasingly difficult depending on your standards.

There is nothing wrong with being picky. If you do not see anyone you're interested in, you can wait longer to see if someone comes that you may wish to play with. You can also chose to be a voyeur for the evening. You can cheer and converse with other people at the party, or you can opt to not participate at all and leave. It's your choice. Do not feel obligated to participate, and do not lower your standards for others. Do what you want, it is your body, and you only do what you can live with.

- **Is it okay for a person to swing without their mate?**

This is entirely up to the couple or swinging partners. I will caution newcomers on leaving your partner during your first couple of parties. There are many reasons why you shouldn't, but the most obvious and most important is to avoid having any problems/issues in the relationship afterward. Again, you have to set the rules for swinging in your relationship, whether you are just swinging partners, in a relationship, boyfriend and girlfriend, or married.

Whatever your particular relationship is, it is important you set and stand by your rules to avoid complications within your relationship.

- **During a threesome, is it okay to cuddle with the invited guest afterward?**

This depends on what your rules are, what your likes and dislikes are, and what you can live with. Some people may consider this as too personal, and a violation of the relationship (cheating). Please understand that just because you were given permission to have sex, you still can cheat, especially if you break rules purposely. If kissing, anal, and/or cuddling is against the rules and you do either of them, then you have just cheated. Again it all depends on the rule(s) of the relationship and what you can live with. (Disclaimer- If you or your partner break a rule that you and/or your partner sets for the party or your relationship, that person has just in fact cheated. Make sure any action is worth the consequences!!!)

• **What would you do to protect my privacy? This question can be directed to your partner or host of a party.**

This is the best question you could possibly ask, and this should be asked to your partner, as well as the party host. I cannot speak for all parties, but as an example, "JFG Enterprises - Formally Known as Swingers Elite of South Atlanta" has adopted a policy of what happens at JFG stays at JFG, Vegas Rules apply and are always in full effect. Parties are not discussed outside of the swingers' club, names are never used, and no staff member discusses the things that go on at the parties with other party goers. There is no photography allowed, including video recording, and all cell phones with a camera must be left in your vehicle. This ensures that no one can get information from a third party, and no mystery pictures of you appear on social media or are mysteriously floating around on the web. If you ask a party host how do they protect your privacy and this is not done at a minimum, then maybe this party is not for you.

With jobs becoming harder to obtain and harder to maintain, it proves to be more critical to protect the personal information that gets out about you. We have all seen where posts on social media sites are more than enough to have someone terminated from a job. Take this into account when deciding to swing as well as personal security.

Personal security does not just mean from physical harm. It includes pictures, rumors, and/or the wrong people having access to your personal information. If you have a great job, you may want to consider whether or not swinging is for you.

The same goes for your partner. Trust is very important and being able to trust your partner that anything you say or do will not leave the party or the comforts of a hotel, house, or where ever you chose to participate is crucial. If you do not feel like you can trust your partner to do this, swinging may not be for you. You may want to think hard about your partner's temperament, meaning if you break up or have disagreements, will your actions still be kept safe between the two of you or will you have to worry about rumors and/or pictures of you getting out. Fortunately, as of summer 2015 it is now a felony to post nude or derogatory pictures of a love one or ex without permission.

- **How should I dress going to a swinger's party?**

Dress code depends on the party. Some parties have dress codes while other parties have a theme such as an all-white party, costume party, etc. If there are no dress codes or themes, then dress nicely. Dress like you are going on a nice date (no suites and ties or Prada necessary), just be casual. I suggest men were khakis and women wear sun dresses or clothing that provide easy access. Sundresses are great for women because they can participate without showing their body, if being shy is an issue.

- **Do people at swingers' parties or during threesomes practice safe sex each time?**

No, however, people should always practice safe sex. Even couples or friends who have sex together should use protection when playing with other couples or an invited guest for a threesome. Again, this is only my suggestion because people do as they want, and some people have a problem commonly referred to as "living in the moment." Don't let a moment change your life.

- **Do gay couples attend swingers' parties?**

Yes, but not to all parties. Typically gay female couples may come to parties, but not often. Male gay couples rarely attend regular swingers' parties. It is not to say that they are not allowed, but socially men partners/couples tend to keep to themselves unless invited by party goers of the same sexual orientation. Parties typically describe which type of orientations will be invited. There are all female parties, parties for only straight, parties for straight and bi, parties for gay only as well as anything goes parties. Find the party that best suits you.

- **Are there rules at a swinger's party or during a threesome?**

At parties yes, refer to chapter 4 for rules for men, women, and couples. In regards to having a threesome, yes there are rules, but the rules are what you make them.

This is in correlation to what your sexual preferences are, and what you and your partner want and expect from each other as well as the invited guest. If you do not speak up, you will not get what you want, and you can get a lot of things you don't want.

- **If it is your first time attending a swingers' party is it best to go with or without your partner?**

Rules, rules, rules. This depends on the rules you establish. I would like to point out that if you feel you have to go without your partner to check it out, then this is an indication that the two of you are not ready to experience this level of openness. One party cannot determine your outlook on all parties as each one is different, some are big and some are small. Some are open to all, where some parties are exclusive. To each their own. Going without each other a few times then coming back and talking about the experiences may work for you and yours. Everyone and every situation is different. Again it is what you can tolerate and live with. I would like to point out that in this instance that I highly discourage going alone for newcomers.

- **What should I expect before, during, or after a threesome?**

Like any first experience you can expect to be nervous before and during. Men, if you have an embarrassing moment, where you cannot perform, it's common, but do not make it a habit. Performance anxiety, along with nervousness, even nausea can occur in men and women. Afterwards, you can expect a flood of emotions. Sometimes people feel ashamed, some feel dirty, some feel free, and some feel liberated and excited. Everyone is different. So how you feel will be based on your own personality and your interpretations of the actions that took place, before, during, and after the threesome.

- **What should I expect before, during or after a swingers' party?**

More or less, the same feelings you experience after a threesome. However, parties are different because you can go and not participate. A good tip is attend your first party just to view, no sex no matter how much you want to. Check out the atmosphere and the tempo of the party. This will let you know if this kind of party is for you. Just because the party is not for you, does not mean swinging isn't for you. It's a process. You will have many feelings, some good and some bad. Just prepare yourself for a new experience and enjoy the ride.

- **Do people get tested for diseases before they come to party?**

The honest answer to this is no, and having sex at a swingers' party is like playing "Russian Rolette." There are some things that a condom will not stop or protect you from.

However, there are some clubs that have strict membership rules, and a clean bill of health has to be proven for membership every other month and HIV/AIDS test have to be done every three months on top of the STD checkups. I personally feel this is a bad thing to do. Why? Because people tend to see HIV free, or STD free, and think that the person that they have sex with is safe. When they think the people they are having sex with are safe, people drop their guard and they allow risky behavior to occur. Please understand, I am not a medical doctor, but I am educated enough to know that some diseases lay dormant for days, weeks, months, even years. This simply means, unless the person you have sex with is your mate, you should always, always use protection. Just in case the answer is unclear, people do not always get tested or know their status. You should always know your status. Before you engage in sex at a party, ask the person if they know their status and what their status is.

- **If you have sex a party will it be private or will there be people watching?**

This depends on the party. Some parties have rooms that are private, and others have an open space. These are things that you should ask the party host, or ask the manager when you go to a sex club. A good party or club will have both open and closed areas so you can have privacy until you are ready to be an exhibitionist.

- **How often do people have parties?**

This depends on the person or group hosting the parties. Some people host once every other month. Some people host once a week. I have run across a few groups that operate like businesses, hosting swingers' parties 3-4 times a week. The same way you come across finding a partner for a threesome, can be used to find people hosting swingers' parties.

- **What areas are popular for swinging parties?**

Believe it or not swingers parties are popular everywhere. It's the types of parties that are rare. One near you may not be your cup of tea, but never the less, swinger's parties and groups are everywhere, nationwide, and not just in urban areas. The key is finding them and becoming associated with them. They are like car clubs, biker gangs, or underground fighting scenes you hear about. You have to find one to know where they are being held. Many sex shops and novelty stores like Adam & Eve, Pricilla's, Star Ships, and Exotic have free newspapers in the front of the store that have locations of swingers' clubs, strip clubs, events, and even personal ads.

- **How do you get comfortable in your own skin when you attend a party?**

There are different ways to adapt to any situation.

Some people like to drink and other people smoke. Whatever you do to deal with a new situation is how and what you should do to get comfortable at a party. I suggest you go early when you are a newcomer. This works great because you won't get stared at when you arrive. You won't be the "fresh meat," and this allows you to look at other people as they arrive. If you are competitive it allows you to size up the competition and if you're shy it allows you to be in control of the situation/environment. Disclaimer: Keshia Green a well-known and respected party host in Southern Atlanta and in the Metro Atlanta Area once said, "Whatever you use to relax or unwind, do so in moderation. Being new and inexperience at a swingers' party is not the place to be incapacitated, you want to be fully coherent in everything around you or pertaining to the party in which you attend."

• **How do you approach people you are interested in?**

With respect. Use the "mother may I" approach. Use this example- "Excuse me miss, I like the way you look. Are you here with someone?" If they say no, ask them if they would like to play. Don't say have sex or fuck, it sounds awkward. If they say they are with someone, you can ask if they are interested in you, and if so do they mind if you asked their partner for permission to play with you.

It would sound like this: "Excuse me miss, I like the way you look. Are you here with someone? Yes. That's awesome. My name is Justin, again I like the way you look. I wanted to know if you would be interested in playing with me, and if so would you mind me asking your partner if it is okay to carry on a conversation with the both of you to see if we can make this happen."

You can also ask the partner they mind if you play or participate without them being present. Closed mouths don't get fed. The "mother may I" approach works great for singles or for couples that see a female/male they would like to play with. This approach gives a polite, courteous, and forward approach to asking for sex/playtime. It even gives a rebuttal for people to use, who you are interested in someone they approached that is attending the party with someone else.

- **How do I find a female or male for a threesome with you and your partner?**

There are many ways to do this:

<u>Internet</u>

There are many sites that advertise sex for people who just want to meet other like-minded people. These sites are different in there functions.

Sites include: Online Booty Call, Adult Friend Finder, Craig's List, Nude Africa, Fling, etc. The point is, the web is full of clubs, sites, and events to search for a suitable third.

Sex clubs

In many states and cities there are swingers' clubs or adult clubs that operate. You can go to these clubs, but usually they require a membership unless you are from out of state. You can usually find out were these swingers'/sex clubs are located by simply using your search engine to locate one near you. GOOGLE IT, "Adult Club or Swingers Club".

Swingers' Parties

Swinger's parties are normally the best way. They are full of people that are like- minded and looking for the same thing. You don't have to participate at the parties if you chose not to.

If you do chose to participate at the party, you don't have to worry about inviting someone to your house, or spending money on a hotel. If inviting someone to your house, going to their house, or even getting a room is not an issue, again this is still the best way to locate a male, female or other couple to participate in playful pleasure with you and/or your partner. You can exchange numbers and information, and get a chance to know the person before you participate.

Ask someone you know

Asking someone you know is easier said than done. When you do this you run the risk of ruining a relationship, whether it's a casual relationship, friendship, or business relationship. This is not recommended unless you are on a level with the person that would lead you to believe that you can even ask such a question. Simply put don't ask unless you already know they are going to say yes and you trust them not to try to run off with your partner.

Ask someone you know, if they know of anyone who would be interested.

Asking someone you know, if they know someone is tricky. This seemingly can be harmless, but this can also be very dangerous to your reputation. Your reputation can easily be damaged unknowingly by people talking about your sexual interest or business. This is particularly dangerous for people with state government, federal, or other white collared jobs where personal life can be a factor in maintaining employment.

Ask someone you don't know.

This is a bold move, and not too many people can pull it off, let alone have the nerve to ask. This is fun and challenging. This will truly build up your self-esteem, especially with a few yes answers under your belt.

• **What do you do when you are interested in a man that is more endowed (larger) than your partner?**

A rule of thumb: If your partner is your boyfriend or man, more importantly if you have feelings for your partner, then do not pursue it. Men are ego driven, and in their mind, they can handle anything. If you have ever seen a man that is sick, then you know that men are quite different on the inside than what we portray on the outside. If you do choose to go larger, it is my opinion to not go over two inches larger. This is because your man has to have sex with you afterward and you do not want a void to be present, or for your walls to be pushed back to where it is untouchable, or to be unable to feel your partner after you get fully wet. These things will create more problems than any relationship can stand. If you have children together, then I am telling you, not warning you, do not do it!

• **What do you do if sex is too good at party?**

There are three ways to answer this. It just depends on which one applies to you.

A) This depends on a few things. Do you have an addictive personality? Do you smoke, drink too much, bite your nails, smoke weed, have an addiction to narcotics? If so, stop while you're ahead. Don't become addicted to sex.

B) If you don't have an addictive personality and the sex was great and you feel guilty, then you can either continue to do it, to see if your feelings towards sex at parties or after having a threesome changes.

C) If you don't feel bad afterwards, have no addictive behaviors, and the sex was just good, then maybe you have found a lifestyle that's good for you. Enjoy your time, continue to be safe, have great sex, and give plenty of great sex back.

- **How do you say no to people during a swingers' party?**

Just as in life, the same goes for swingers' parties or events, everyone has the right to say "No." We all know through life experiences that there are different strokes for different folks, which means, everybody is not right for everybody else. This is fine.
You may want someone who doesn't want you, and someone could want you, and you don't want them. Improper handling of a situation, however, can lead to a lot of hurt or very bad feelings. To answer the question, it can and should be done with a simple, "No, thank you." Never give an explanation because that is what usually causes the problems.
- **Why is it important to be nice to everyone at a swinger's party?**

Whether or not you are personally interested in swinging with someone, be polite. You never know who you may meet. It could be a new friend, a new partner or even your mate. It could be a like-minded business associate or business partner. You never know, most power deals are handled in strip clubs, so it's not far-fetched that you could meet someone that could become significant in your life from attending a party or event. Don't miss out on life changing experiences, moments, or even fate because of a bad attitude.

The purpose of this chapter is to answer some tough and common questions. It is also to reiterate that anything that happens is because of what you chose to let happen. I have repeatedly stated that you have to set rules, follow your rules, and only do what you can live with.

Summary

After reading this book, some people will know exactly what they want to do and how to do it. They will know if swinging is a lifestyle that they want to partake in, or if it is not for them, while others will ask their friends' opinions, ear mark parts of the book, then go back over the book again to finally sleeping on it, awake and still have no decision. It is a hard decision for most people to make. It can be life altering in so many ways, some for the good and some for the bad. As discussed before, it can rejuvenate your relationship or it can tear it apart. So what do you do if after talking to your partner, evaluating if swinging is for you, and at the end of the book you still don't know if you want to participate or not? I have the solution for you!

This may sound odd, and may be a little extreme for some, but to get a feel for swinging without having to swing, you will have to give yourself the opportunity to pre-swing or preview swinging in action with no pressure. In order to accomplish this, I would like for you to host two adult swingers' parties either at a residence or at a hotel. These parties will illustrate the six rules to abide by, along with the dos and don'ts located in Chapter 3, Party Etiquette. You need to see the different types of people who come out to participate. I know that is vague, but trust me, it will be self-explanatory after the party. Do not charge admission to the parties.

The first party will be a regular (non-themed) event. This means no dress code with no mask required and pretty much come as you are.

For the second party you will implement some rules. Some examples of rules would be stating that party masks are required and there would be a cut off time for arrival/entry.

Now you may ask, why would you have these two types of parties? The answer is to gain knowledge.

Party 1: At this party you will have all types, shapes, and orientations invited. This will let you see the different types of people who come out to the parties.

Party 2: This party is going to be fun, exciting, and a pain in the ass. For the most part, it will go smoothly, but you will have people who just cannot seem to get it together. You will have people that believe they are privileged and think they do not have to follow your set rules, like wearing a mask for example. You will even have some to totally ignore your rules and come to the party with no mask. It is up to you to let them enter or not. I advise *not* because the other party goers will want to take their masks off, or they may be offended that you have people there who are not wearing masks. You will have others that will go out of their way to defy your rules. If you say don't go in the kitchen they will sneak into the kitchen. If you say don't go into a room or not to use a particular restroom that will be the room that they sneak off to.

While hosting, have games ready for people to play, have ice breakers and serve drinks. Be a good host, but do not participate. When you participate you lose sight of what's going on in your surroundings. Remember, hosting a party is a big deal and can easily become overwhelming. The purpose of having you host your own party is to observe all the things that go on within the context of the party. Observe how the men leave their partners to sneak off and do their own thing, and how the women do the same. Observe how couples get caught up, the arguments and fights that occur. Look at the people who are nervous versus the ones who let loose. Observe the ones that drink too much, and fully indulge themselves in the environment knowing full well that they will regret what they did next in the morning. Feel the pressures of hosting and of trying to control an environment which is not meant to be controlled. People come to parties to explore, let lose, and escape the confines of social control, but as a host, you have to hold the reins and steer your party in the direction you want it to go. Being able to let lose is great, but as a host you have to have some control over the environment. If you haven't guessed by now, you are responsible for the things that go on and the things that go wrong at a party. These are learning tools. Use these parties as assessment guidelines for what you want and don't want to happen to you or someone you have sex with. Use the party to gain a little insight and a little more knowledge into the swinging lifestyle.

If you are still not sure at this point, refer back to the first chapter, first paragraph. Just dive in or make an informed decision. In my opinion, if you have made it to this point and you are not sure, I believe it is safe to say that swinging is not for you. Now on the other hand, if you have made it to this point and you have followed guidelines in the summary including hosting parties, and observed all the things that others do or don't do, and you still think you are ready to swing, then I say go for it. Please make sure you understood the rules and know the potential consequences, but don't step one foot inside the lifestyle of a swinger until you have you are fully prepared to open Pandora's Box and understand *The Art of Swinging...*

The End!

Appendix A

Before you swing ask yourself...

Questions you and/or your partner should ask yourselves and each other. Please read, write your answers down, and discuss your responses honestly.

• Why do we want to start this lifestyle; swinging or threesomes?

• What does swinging mean to me?

• Do I feel like I am being pressured, bullied, or coerced into swinging or to have threesomes?

• Am I thinking about swinging as a way out of this relationship?

• Do I want to have sex with other people because I am unsatisfied with my partner(s)?

• Do I want to have sex with other people because I'm bored sexually?

• What am I most afraid of happening when I think of us, or my partner swinging?

• Do I believe that the act of sex can be distinctly separated from love and intimacy?

• Am I considering swinging because there's a person in particular that I want to be sexually intimate with?

• Is swinging a way to "cheat" on my partner without feeling like I'm really cheating?

• Do we want to engage in swinging or threesomes as a way of rejuvenating the sexual stimulation we once had in our relationship?

• Do I want to engage in swinging to see if, "I still got it?"

• Does swinging mean full penetration or something else?

• Is kissing okay during a party, threesome, or while swinging?

• Is cuddling after sex okay with an invited guest or with other couple we decide to have sex with?

• Is anal sex okay during a party, threesome, or while swinging?

• Is oral sex okay? If we agree to perform oral sex on other people, does a condom or dental dam need to be used?

• Do we need to have condoms or dental dams used on us when other people perform oral sex on us?

• Will we always use condoms, even if we decide to have a boyfriend/girlfriend?

• Will we always swing together in the same room, in different rooms, or both?

• If we have a threesome, will it always be a team effort, or will there be one- on-one play time with the invited guest?

• If one of us wants to stop swinging for whatever reason, can we mutually accept that decision?

• What will I not tolerate? What will we not tolerate?

• Do we agree to not discuss personal matters about us with whoever we swing with?

• How do I define jealousy? Am I a jealous person?

• Should feelings of jealousy be a reason to stop swinging?

• Am I emotionally ready for swinging or having a threesome?

• What will happen if I get pregnant by someone else we swing with?

• Will you support me if I have someone else's baby? What would you have me do?

• Will you support me I have an abortion or give the child up for adoption?

• Am I okay with having an abortion or giving a child up for adoption?

• If I keep the baby, what do we tell our family and friends? Can we really live with this?

• Do I have any STD's or infections that I am aware of?

• Do the people we swing with have STD's? Should we have them get tested?

- Should I tell people if I have (or if we have) any STD's, now or in the past?

- Will we swing with the same people always, or will it be different people each time?

- Outside of sex what do we define as "getting to close" to the people we swing with?

- Can we regularly have times that are set aside just for us, that doesn't include swinging?

- What do I hope to gain from this experience after we swing for the first time?

- Are we still in love with each other? If not, do you think this will help? If so, do you think this will hurt us?

How was it? Not easy, huh? These questions are not meant to be easy. They are meant to be hard, difficult, and designed to make you think hard and long before you dive in. Swinging is fun, but there are consequences. Things happen, and the purpose of these set of questions are to give you the tools and knowledge needed to make an informed decision. You will not be able to say you were not prepared if you read this book. Answer the questions honestly, think about them and your feelings towards the answers, and discuss your answers together.

Appendix B

Glossary

*note terms are the sole opinion of the author, and are meant to give the reader a grasp on various terms that one my see or hear in the lifestyle; not in alphabetical order.

Kink Positivity- An attitude towards human sexuality that embraces the full diversity of all safe consensual sexual activities as fundamentally healthy and pleasurable, and acknowledges that there is nothing immoral or shameful about non-conventional forms of sexual expression.

Lifestyle- term used to describe persons who are like minded and engaged in adult activities as described above in the term "kink positivity".

Swinger- married couple that engages in adult activities as described above in the term "kink positive". Originally meant for couple for couple activities, the term has since evolved to involve other facets of sexual expression.

Vanilla- Term used to describe persons who are not in the lifestyle.

Newbies- Term used to describe persons who are new to the lifestyle with little to no experience.

Bi-Occasional- Not to be confused with bi-curious, bi-selective, or bi-sexual. A term used to describe men or women who occasionally "Rarely" engage in sexual activities with persons of the same sex. That do not view themselves as bisexual.

Dress Down- Term used to describe time set aside during a party for participating guests to change into undergarments, i.e. lingerie/sexy wear signifying a change in tempo usually going from casual conversation to "play time" (Dress down is not always mandatory, but always encouraged)

Host-(a) A person who caters to those he/she invites over to their home or meeting place for a social occasion (i.e. adult party)

(b) The ability to have someone visit your home for a private encounter ("You said you do not play at parties. So are you able to host at your house?)

Polyamorous "Poly"- Term used to describe a committed relationship between three or more persons. Not to be confused with the act of having sex with three or more persons i.e. 3sum, orgy, gangbang. This term is solely used to describe a relationship that is more than just sexually based.

Play/Play time- Term used to suggest and ask for sexual contact or intercourse. Term used as a light hearted euphemism instead of bluntly asking a person to have sex, give head, or Fuck. (In a swingers party setting-Hi my name is Alex, notice you setting there, was wondering if you would like to Play with me in the other room?)

Unicorn- Mythical creators that are majestic and rare; term coincides with females that are bi-sexual and can get along with couple evenly and long enough to satisfy both partners without upsetting the balance of the relationship. The term is given because finding a female that can do so is extremely rare, and is looked upon as being a mystical and magical entity that its self can only be described as a fairytale.

Thoroughbred- A term used to describe what was once called a couples boy toy. This term describes the male version of unicorn. Though not mythical, these bi males are rare and hard to come by. Being able to supplement what's needed in the relationship by being able to plays roles such as the alpha male as well as a subordinate/submissive partner. Not to be confused with a Stallion. (Coined by Justin Green 2013)

Stallion- A term used to describe a male that is similar to a thoroughbred, these males however are not bi-sexual but are able to interact with a couple in a way that does not break the harmonious and delicate balance of the relationship; whether its inside or outside of the bedroom. Stallions are not rare, however couples that are willing to engage with stallions or thoroughbreds are rare. (Coined by Justin Green 2013)

T.H.O.T- That hoe over there; synonym- Ratchet; term used to describe a female that is looked upon by others in a way that is unfitting to be labeled as a respectable woman. This term replaced words such as hoe, wore, bitch, slut, skank and husset "hussy"; and combined them into one acronym. Women referred to under this term are commonly disruptive and unprofessional/disrespectful at social gathering and private settings.

Bootydo- A term used to describe a female with a stomach that exceeds at length, the length of her buttocks. (Your stomach stick out more than your booty do! booty-do)

Camel Toe- A. Term used to describe the vaginal area of a female. A woman said to have camel toe, has two pronounced labia's (vaginal lips). So much so that when said vagina is seen in or through panties or in tight pants that it resembles the toe of a Camel.

B. Camel toe is normally the result of a woman who wears tight paints, tights and/or leggins that are pulled upward to the extent that they are pressed up against the crouch entering in between the labia's (Vaginal Lips). The impression of the paints against the crouch and in between the labia create the shape that resembles a camel's toe.

BBW- Term used to describe and label plus size women. The term stands for Big and Beautiful Women. Term usually commonly reserved for women sizes 16 and larger (American sizes).

Pansexual- Not limited in sexual choice with regard to biological sex, gender, or gender identity. This term refers to a person that has no sexual preference that can have sex with, mate with, and even love persons of other sexual classifications i.e. transgendered, male, female, androgynous.

Fetish- A term that refers to an obsession or attraction to things that can be sexual or non-sexual that cause sexual arousal.

Algolagnia- A term used to describe sexual acts of sexuoeroticism that is contingent on receiving physical pain, in particular in the erogenous zone. Not to be confused with sexual sadism or masochism, which is sexual gratification from inflicting pain.

P2P- Pay to Play- Term commonly used by professional women (Prostitutes) in layman's terms you have to pay the person to have sex or sexual encounters with them. Note if they say you are paying for time or companionship this still means the same thing that you are in fact paying to have sex. You can be arrested for this act if caught.

Jump Off- A derogatory term used to describe women that people "use" for sexual gratification, while unknowingly being the victim of mental and sexual manipulation.

Party-Starter/ Ice Breaker- A term used to describe a person who is unmoved by crowds of people, and not scared to be the "First one/person" to engage in sexual activities during a party or event. Action also commonly referred to as an ice breaker. Not to be confused with jump' off.

Note: Although most who do not know the true definition of the term commonly refer to Party-Starters as "Jump-Offs".

Ice Breakers- A term used to describe actions taken to relieve some anxiety in guest that attend parties or events. Actions can also be taken to liven up a situation. Actions normally include either; Introductions or Games,

Friends with Benefits (FWB)-Term used to describe a relationship between friends that have casual sex.

Playmate- Term used to describe a person that you engage in intercourse or sexual activities with, that also shares the benefits of having no boundaries or limitations while playing with one another. In short; No title while receiving wife/husband/spousal benefits in the bedroom.

NSA- No Strings Attached- Term used to describe casual sex that afterwards, has no meaning, feelings, or attachments. Can be once or an ongoing arrangement. Similar to friends with benefits

Pillow Princess- Term used to describe a female that derives pleasure from receiving pleasure and not giving pleasure. It is a common misconception that pillow princesses are lazy sex partners (lazy lay), But the term originally spans from a female of regal status or heritage that invokes the privilege of not having to reciprocate sexual acts

P4H (Play for Him)-Term used to describe a relationship where the female plays and/or has sex with other men or women for her partner. The woman either records the acts, takes pictures of the acts, writes the acts down in detail, or describes the sexual acts to and/or for her mate. The male derives pleasure from either hearing the act occur, seeing the act, or talking about the sexual act. (This usually occurs when couples are forced to be separated from one another i.e. Incarcerated, Deployment, etc.) (Coined by Justin Green 2013)

Netflick'n (watching Netflix)- Term used to describe a casual way of asking for sex. Sex is usually paired with some type of initiation of viewing a movie that ends with what was thought to be spontaneous sex. Similar to someone asking a person to play. (Coined by Keshia Green 2013) **Note: If someone ask you to come over to watch Netflix, they are more than likely using a paraphrase. They usually mean Netflick'n.**

Cuffing- A term used to describe a temporary relationship. Not seen or viewed as a real relationship. It is seemingly a relationship during "Cuffing Season" that has no official title.

Cuffing Season- A term used to describe a period of time usually starting in the fall and ending 2-3 weeks before spring. Synonymous with cuffing.

Tax Season- Term used to describe a period of months roughly November to May; where a man physically and mentally manipulates a female or females, he perceives are going to receive large State and Federal refund checks (single females with multiple children), in an attempt to sway the female into taking care of the man financially while benefiting from sex as well. Can include but is not limited to buying items for man, paying man's bills, and/or even given the man money directly. Cuffing is usually the preferred technique to accomplish this. (Coined by Justin Green 2013)

Bottom- Male that derives pleasure from having intercourse through anal penetration instead of using his penis to have sex. Term is also used in professional role as a male that has sex anally for money. Man may or may not be bi-sexual or gay.

Top- Male that derives pleasure from having intercourse with another male through the means of penetration of the male's anus. Term is also used in professional role as a man that has sex with other males for money. Man may or may not be bi-sexual or gay.

Versatile "Verse"- Male that derives pleasure from having sex through anal penetration as well as having the ability to perform and derive pleasure from using his penis to have sex through means of penetration of another man's anus. Termed is also used in professional role as man that has sex with other males for money and that can perform both roles as a top and bottom.

BDSM- stands for Bondage and Discipline, Domination and submission, Sadism and Masochism.

S&M- Slave and Master

BBC- Big Black Cock/Penis

T4M- Transsexual seeking the company of men

M4M- Male seeking the company of other men

W4M- Women seeking the company of men

W4W- Women seeking the company of other women

ME4M- Couple seeking 3sum with another male

MW4W- Couple seeking 3sum with another female

MW4T- Couple seeking 3sum with a Transsexual

MW4MW- Couple seeking company of another couple

CD- Cross dresser

BYOB- Bring your own beverage/beer/bottle

BYOC- Bring your own condoms/contraceptives (hygiene items are normally encouraged as well)

MFM- Threesome that describes the ratio of men to woman as 2 to 1. In these explanation, there are two men whose purpose is to please the female in the described ratio. The middle letter (F) indicating which person is the focus of the encounter.

FFM/MFF- Threesome that described the ratio of men to woman as 1 to 2. In this explanation, there are two women and one man, the man and women purpose is to please the female. The middle letter (F) indicating which person is the focus of the encounter.

FMF- Threesome that describes the ration of men to woman as 1 to 2. In this explanation, there are two women whose purpose is to please the male in the described ratio. The middle letter (M) indicating which person is the focus of the encounter.

Exhibitionist -A person or persons who enjoys having sexual encounters in public places (can be at adult party or outside of a party "public") and is aroused at the possibility of being seen or caught in the act.

Squirting- (controversial term) Term that describes the orgasm of a woman that releases a large amount of fluid during the peak of her climax (controversial because some believe that squirting is the act of a woman urinating during sex as a result of intense pleasure that relaxes the bladder muscles and allows the body to relax in such a state that fluid is released from the bladder and expelled during the climax; while others believe this is the female version of ejaculating. To add to the controversy, some believe the fluid comes from the vaginal opening while others believe it comes from the urethra.)

Adult Party/ Meet & Greets- Term that describes a gathering that consists of adults (18 years of age or older). This party does not always include sex but can/may lead to it. Party is usually a non-sexual party.

Lifestyle party- Term that describes an adult party consisting of like-minded individuals and couples. These can be a social gathering or extravagant events. The premise of the party is sex and the possibility of having sex is there. Rooms and areas for play are set aside for those who wish to play. Playing is not mandatory. Playing may or may not be expected, but always accepted without judgement.

Swingers Party- Term used to describe an adult party that sex is more of the primary objective than the actual party itself. The party is a prop for the center stage of potential sex. The party give a distraction and a brace for the ability to pace one's self at the party. The full intent is to have sex at this party, but is not mandatory. However it is custom to know that this party is for sex and any advances should not be taken as disrespect but as a gesture that you are a suitable mate to engage in sexual intercourse with. (In layman's terms do not be mad if multiple people ask you for sex or different forms of sex at this party)

Sex/Fuck Party- Term used to describe an adult party that sex is the only objective. This party usually consist of a small to medium number of people usually between 5-20 persons. The guest are usually screened and known by the host if not the majority of the guest there. Sometimes there is a casual setting area to allow for conversation or breaks during party; but this is not always the case due to the environmental and nature of the party. (Laymen's terms- you're not there to talk, your there to get it in)

Gang Bang(s)- Term used to describe intercourse with 3 or more persons with one willing partner. Note; if person is unwilling the act is called Gang Rape

Orgy- Term used to describe sex between 5 or more persons at the same place over a period of the same time.

Anything Goes Party (pansexual Party)- This party is the sitting of sexual encounters of various forms. The term means exactly how it's read, men on men, men on women, BDSM, Furies, satanic play, whips, flogging, etc. Best to ask what the patrons are normally into before attending.

Water Play/Water Sports- Term used to describe sexual activity in which urine is involved. The presence of urine is generally considered erotic for those indulging in the urine related activities. Water sports can include other fluids such as, saliva and blood. This is considered "edge-play" because it is obviously somewhat unhygienic.

Pegging- Term used to describe the action of a woman using a dildo/strap to insert in and used to have sex with a male; anally?

Voyeurism- The term used to describe a person that derives sexual gratification from watching the sexual acts of others in person i.e. "Live Porn."

Cream Pie- Term used to describe the act of ejaculating inside a vagina or rectum and the moment after wards when the sperm drips out.

MoneyShot- Term used to describe a man ejaculating on a woman's Face, Breast, Pelvic area or Buttock. Signifying the completion of sexual act with great pleasure.

Bukkake- Term used to describe a fetish that involves repeated ejaculation on a person by many men.

Vegas Rules- What happens at an adult party stays at an adult party.

Analingus/39- The term used to describe the act of one person licking another person anus, now commonly referred to as "Eating Groceries" The number is a depiction or Emoticon that denotes analingus. Turned on its side, the 3 becomes butt cheeks, the 9 becomes a smiling mouth with tongue.

69- The term used to describe simultaneous oral sex between two people. This can be achived with 2 males, 2 females, or most commonly 1 male and 1 female. The number references the inverted versions of each number, reflecting the physical position that the 2 persons must adopt when engaged in this sexual practice.

GG/Girl-Girl/Girl on Girl- Term used to describe sex between two or more females where males watch without Participating or interacting with females. Not to be confused with Partial swap or Soft Swap.

Partial Swap- Term used to describe sex between two couples where only the females swap, and the males have sex with their original partners

Soft Swap- Term used to describe a form of sexual acts between two willing couples. Penetrations is not performed only oral copulation

Full Swap- Term used to describe sex between two couples that change partners during the course of intercourse.

Xenophile/xenophilia- Term used to describe a person's sexual attraction to things which are different or towards the unknown.

Bare Back- Describes a term for sexual intercourse without a condom

Hall Pass- Term used to describe the issuance of permission from one partner to the other, allowing the partner that has received the pass to have sex with another person(s) for a set limit of time.

420 Friendly- Term used to describe the acceptance of drugs at a party or event. In most cases this is only meant to mean weed or spice (synthetic weed). But in recent times, the term has broadened to include the use of all drugs to include recreational and hard drugs. **Note: Be sure to check with the host of any adult situation to see what 420 means to them and what substances outside of alcohol are permitted at the party/event whether it be private or intimate setting.**

Acknowledgements

Angela Green- Thank you for loving me and supporting me with everything I do; for helping me even when I don't want you to. All women are compared to you. I love you

Keshia N. Green- Richland GA/ Atlanta GA - **Co-Author, Editing, Love, Sponsorship, Friendship and support.-Loving Wife.**

Elaine Jakes- Conyers GA, **Casandra Barlow-** Jonesboro GA, **Latisha Smith-Mitchell-** Raleigh NC, **Rodrick Rogers-** Atlanta GA, **Anthony Berry-** Atlanta GA, **Angie Hensley-** Union City GA, **Ramona Campbell-** New Haven CT, **Rick Brown-** Atlanta GA, **Leah Ephram-** San Antonio TX, **Sondra Booker-** San Antonio TX* **Friendship and Support. Thank you.**

Kenya Davis- Fayetteville NC, **Rochelle Hawkins-** Washington DC, **Joy Wiggs-** Goldsboro NC, **Anthony Hammond-** Fayetteville NC, **Kieona Manning-**Dillon SC* **Family, Friendship, Love and Support**

Caressia Edwards- Fayetteville NC; **Love, Support, Lessons Learned, Great Friend/Lover.**

Cynthia V. Carney- Riverdale MD; **Thank you for supporting me in all I do, Lover, Editing, Lessons Learned.**

Chrishonda Nikkiya Ham- Wilson NC/Fayetteville NC; **Vanilla as they come. Hope you remain that way. Pure and sweet; you are the sweetest, warmest, and kindhearted person i know or have ever met. Love you**

thank you for being my "Best Friend." You have always been there when I needed you most. THANK YOU!

Tracy Truit- DownTown Silver Springs MD; **Thanks for Editing, Friendship, Love and Support.**

Christel D. Bryant- Fayetteville NC; **For Financial Support, friendship, love I didn't deserve, Lover, having my back even through the Bull.**

Yoland V. Fuller ; Formally Kouassi- Fayetteville NC; **Friendship & Exceptional bedroom performance. Saintified Monster in bed, Friend for Ever #the one that got away.**

Erica Armstrong- Atlanta Ga; **Thank you for being a friend. Having my back and our back.**

Aisha F. Newman A.k.A Carmelz Delights- Fayetteville NC; **Thanks for being a friend and a special lover. Our first unicorn, living proof that fairytales do come true.**

Nashuma Knight Atlanta GA/Fayetteville NC. **Beautiful inside and out. A friend, a companion and so much more, in so many ways. We both love you.**

Ebony Green, Nikia Perry, Amanda Brewer- For your **hard work, continuous dedication, loyalty and concern. All of you have a portion of my heart and a product of my soul. Thank you three the most. You have gave me legacy**

***Special Thanks to the two women in my life that have defined me as a man and help mode me through the years. My failures, my accomplishments, my very existence has been shaped by these two women. My Ex-wife, and my Wife:

Ebony Green- Fayetteville NC; Special enough to be mentioned twice. 15 years, all I can say is thank you. Lessons learned, will always love you and have love for you. Thanks for making me a better man.

Lakeshia N. Green- Formally Britton. Atlanta GA- You have given me new hope, new light, new reason. You trust me, you encourage me. You inspire me to be more. All things I do are for you, us, my kids and finally myself. I owe you so much more than I could ever return or inspire to repay. You are a woman's woman, and the pillar of my heart. Thank you for being my wife, my best friend, and my partner. I love you.

***To the people who make swinging a lifestyle and not just sex-

John "Cuddi" Baker & Takita "Pecan Thick" Barlow: Cuddi's World & Erotic Atlanta Vibes "EAV"

Jon & Cynthia: Couples Retreat & Soul to Soul & Couples Retreat Remix

Meezy Numbers, Blakk the Mayor, Long Hook: The commission

Long Hook and Jersey Gyrl: Freaks4 Life

Ben and Lasonja Shaw: Benz Promotions

TP: Group Leader for Ultimate Pleasures

Grand Mistress: Mistressville

Christoria Rhodes "Risqué Williams": Tap out Team & All About Tha Lifestyle

Keisha "Lipzz" Reeves: Cummrez n Twatterz

Ebonie Burks Taylor: My sexy Bubbles

If I have forgotten to list you, charge it to my mind, not my heart.

***Last, but not least I would like to say thank you to Aishah Flood- Atlanta, GA and Right Circle Publications for giving me a chance to share my thoughts with the world. THANK YOU & Thank you to the rest of the owners of Right Circle Publications.

Are you an aspiring author, or current author looking for a publishing home? Well great news! Right Circle Publications is currently ACCEPTING SUBMISSIONS.

Guidelines:
-First 3-5 Chapters
-Synopsis & Title (If Known)
-Contact Information (including Social Media)
Please send submissions to:
rightcirclepublications@yahoo.com
Please allow 3-5 business days for a response